A CourseGuide for

Grasping God's Word

J. Scott Duvall
J. Daniel Hays

ZONDERVAN ACADEMIC

A CourseGuide for Grasping God's Word
Copyright © 2020 by Zondervan

Requests for information should be addressed to:
Zondervan, *3900 Sparks Dr. SE, Grand Rapids, Michigan 49546*

ISBN 978-0-310-11016-3 (softcover)

All Scripture quotations, unless otherwise indicated, are taken from The Holy Bible, New International Version®, NIV®. Copyright © 1973, 1978, 1984, 2011 by Biblica, Inc.® Used by permission of Zondervan. All rights reserved worldwide. www.Zondervan.com. The "NIV" and "New International Version" are trademarks registered in the United States Patent and Trademark Office by Biblica, Inc.®

Any internet addresses (websites, blogs, etc.) and telephone numbers in this book are offered as a resource. They are not intended in any way to be or imply an endorsement by Zondervan, nor does Zondervan vouch for the content of these sites and numbers for the life of this book.

No part of this publication may be reproduced, stored in a retrieval system, or transmitted in any form or by any means — electronic, mechanical, photocopy, recording, or any other — except for brief quotations in printed reviews, without the prior permission of the publisher.

Printed in the United States of America

CONTENTS

Introduction 5

1. Bible Translations 7
2. The Interpretive Journey 11
3. How to Read the Book: Sentences 15
4. How to Read the Book: Paragraphs 19
5. How to Read the Book: Discourses 23
6. The Historical-Cultural Context 27
7. What Do We Bring to the Text? 31
8. The Literary Context 35
9. Word Studies 39
10. Who Controls the Meaning? 43
11. Levels of Meaning 47
12. The Role of the Holy Spirit 50
13. Application 54
14. New Testament: Letters 58
15. New Testament: Gospels 62
16. New Testament: Acts 66
17. New Testament: Revelation 70

18. **Old Testament: Narrative** 74

19. **Old Testament: Law** 77

20. **Old Testament: Poetry** 81

21. **Old Testament: Prophets** 85

22. **Old Testament: Wisdom** 89

Introduction

Welcome to *A CourseGuide for Grasping God's Word*. These guides were created for formal and informal students alike who want to engage deeper in biblical, theological, or ministry studies. We hope this guide will provide an opportunity for you to grow not only in your understanding, but also in your faith.

How to Use This Guide

This guide is meant to be used in conjunction with the book *Grasping God's Word* and its corresponding videos, *Grasping God's Word Video Lectures*. After you have read each chapter in the book and watched the accompanying video lesson, the materials in this guide will help you review and assess what you have learned. Application-oriented questions are included as well. For additional practice, you will want to complete exercises found in *Grasping God's Word Workbook*.

Each CourseGuide has been individually designed to best equip you in your studies, but in general, you can expect the following components. Most CourseGuides begin every chapter with a "You Should Know" section, which highlights key terminology, people, and facts to remember. This section serves as a helpful summary for directing your studies. Reflection questions, typically two to three per chapter, prompt you to summarize key points you've learned. Discussion questions invite you to an even deeper level of engagement. Finally, most chapters will end with a short quiz to test your retention. You can find the answer key to each quiz at the bottom of the page following it.

For Further Study

CourseGuides accompany books and videos from some of the world's top biblical and theological scholars. They may be used independently, or in small groups or classrooms, offering quality instruction to equip students for academic and ministry pursuits. If you would like to engage in further study with Zondervan's CourseGuides, the full lineup may be viewed online. After completing your studies with *A CourseGuide for Grasping God's Word*, we recommend moving on to *A CourseGuide for How to Read the Bible for All Its Worth* and *A CourseGuide for Introduction to Biblical Interpretation*.

CHAPTER 1

Bible Translations

You Should Know

- Out of whose mouth did Scripture come—God's or man's? The only biblical answer is "both." Indeed, God spoke through the human authors in such a way that their words were simultaneously his.

- Scripture is equally the Word of God and the words of human beings. Better, it is the word of God through the words of human beings. Through inspiration God used various human authors to write the Bible.

- Translation entails "reproducing the meaning of a text that is in one language (the source language), as fully as possible, in another language (the receptor language)."

- Characteristics of the formal approach: attempts to maintain structure of source language; less sensitive to the receptor language, which may result in an awkward translation; approaches to translating God's Word

- Characteristics of the functional approach: a thought-for-thought approach, which focuses on today's language; less sensitive to the source language, which may result in distorted meaning since form helps communicate meaning

- Translation: transferring the message of one language into another language

- Biblical translation: transferring God's message found in the pages of the Bible, which was originally written in Hebrew and Greek, into your language

- Paraphrase: not a translation, but a restatement of a particular English translation using different English words

Essay Questions

Short

1. How can we be certain that the Bible we possess is God's Word? What exactly does it mean to be God's Word?

2. What makes a good Bible translation? Discuss some key steps in choosing a Bible translation.

3. Why is a Bible paraphrase not recommended for serious Bible study?

Long

1. How is the Bible both God's Word and man's word? Explain and defend your response.

Quiz

1. (T/F) Textual criticism is a discipline that compares various biblical texts to determine what is most likely the original.

2. (T/F) In hindsight, the KJV was not a very good translation, even in 1611.

3. (T/F) A paraphrase is not technically a translation since it does not translate from the original languages, but instead restates an English translation.

4. (T/F) One guideline to use in choosing a Bible translation is one that gives preference to a translation by an individual rather than a committee.

5. Which of the following is *NOT* a challenge that faces contemporary readers of the King James Version.

a) The KJV is based on only a few later Greek manuscripts.
b) The KJV uses archaic English that makes it difficult to read.
c) The KJV Old Testament was based upon the Greek Septuagint.
d) None of the above

6. Which of the following is *NOT* an example of what makes translation difficult in light of the fact that no two languages are alike:

   a) No two *words* are alike.
   b) The vocabulary of any two languages will vary in size.
   c) Languages have different stylistic preferences.
   d) We do not possess the original manuscripts for proper comparison.

7. Regarding types of Bible translation, a more _____ approach tries to stay as close as possible to the structure and words of the source language.

   a) Formal
   b) Functional
   c) Literal
   d) Allegorical

8. Regarding types of Bible translation, a more _____ approach tries to express the meaning of the original text in today's language.

   a) Formal
   b) Functional
   c) Literal
   d) Allegorical

9. Which of the following contemporary Bible translations would be an example of one that follows the translation approach that tries to stay as close as possible to the structure and words of the source language?

   a) *The Message*
   b) NLT
   c) NIV
   d) NASB

10. Which of the following contemporary Bible translations would be an example of one that follows the translation approach that tries to express the meaning of the original text in today's language?

  a) KJV
  b) HCSB
  c) NLT
  d) ESV

ANSWER KEY

1. T, 2. F, 3. T, 4. F, 5. C, 6. D, 7. A, 8. B, 9. D, 10. C

CHAPTER 2

The Interpretive Journey

You Should Know

- Three methods of biblical interpretation: intuitive or feels-right approach; Spiritualizing Approach; Shrug Your Shoulders Approach

- Step 1: Grasping the Text in Their Town — Question: What did the text mean to the biblical audience?

- Completing Step 1: read the text carefully and make observations; study the historical and literary context; synthesize the meaning of the passage for the biblical audience

- Step 2: Measuring the Width of the River to Cross — Question: What are the differences between the biblical audience and us?

- Completing Step 2: account for common differences: culture, language situation, time and covenant; focus on the unique differences found in a specific text; if you are studying an Old Testament passage, you must account for the life and work of Jesus Christ

- Step 3: Crossing the Principalizing Bridge — Question: What is the theological principle in this text?

- Completing Step 3: recall the differences identified in Step 2; identify any similarities between the biblical audience and contemporary life; holding the differences and similarities together, identify a broad theological principle

- A theological principle should be reflected in the text, be timeless and not tied to a specific situation, not be culturally bound, correspond to the teaching of the rest of Scripture, and be relevant to both the biblical and contemporary audience.

- Step 4: Consult the Biblical Map — Question: How does our theological principle fit with the rest of the Bible?

- Completing Step 4: Does this principle correlate with the rest of the Bible? If in the Old Testament, run your theological principle through the grid of the New Testament.

- Step 5: Grasping the Text in Our Town — Question: How should individual Christians today live out the theological principles?

- Completing Step 5: Apply the theological principle to the specific situation of a contemporary Christian; there are numerous applicable possibilities, because Christians today find themselves in a variety of situations.

Essay Questions

Short

1. What elements can provide a direct barrier between the biblical text and application today?

2. Discuss the importance of approaching the Bible to first understand its meaning and then apply it to our lives today.

3. How is a theological principle derived from a passage? How can a theological principle help in our understanding of the meaning of a passage and also provide a way for application?

Long

1. Describe the five steps in the Interpretive Journey.

Quiz

1. (T/F) A major element to consider in how we approach interpreting the New Testament in contrast with the Old Testament is a change in covenant.

2. (T/F) If the specifics of a particular text of Scripture only apply to the particular situation of a biblical audience, there is no direct contemporary application that can be drawn.

3. (T/F) When drawing a theological principle from a text, we must be certain that the principle is culturally bound.

4. (T/F) Theological principles should correspond to the teaching of the rest of Scripture.

5. Even when studying the New Testament, the different _____, language, and specific situations can present a barrier to our desire to grasp the meaning of a text.

    a) Authors
    b) Purpose
    c) Culture
    d) None of the above

6. The _____ approach to Bible interpretation incorrectly interprets Scripture in such a way that if a text looks as though it can be directly applied, then we attempt to do so.

    a) Conservative
    b) Feels-right approach
    c) Literal
    d) Philosophical

7. The main goal to keep in mind is to grasp the _____ of the text God has intended.

    a) Meaning
    b) Application
    c) Principle
    d) None of the above

8. The first step in accurately understanding a passage of Scripture is to _____.

    a) Conduct a word study on significant words
    b) Read the text
    c) Make observations
    d) Look for repeated words or phrases

9. Before we can accurately understand how to apply a text, we need to determine _____.

   a) Who the author was
   b) Its overall context
   c) What it meant to the original audience
   d) The theological principles

10. In order to determine a theological principle of a passage, we need to be certain that the principle is _____ in the text.

   a) Reflected
   b) Hidden
   c) Time-sensitive to the original readers
   d) Tied to a specific situation

ANSWER KEY

1. T, 2. F, 3. F, 4. T, 5. C, 6. B, 7. A, 8. B, 9. C, 10. A

CHAPTER 3

How to Read the Book: Sentences

You Should Know

- Repetition of words: Look for words that repeat. How many times is this word repeated in the immediate context? Is this word repeated in the wider context? Does the repeated word always serve the same function? Does the repeated word utilize the same meaning each time it occurs?

- Things to look for in sentences
  - Contrast: Look for items, ideas, or individuals that are contrasted. What word signals the contrast? What ideas, individuals, or items are being contrasted?
  - Comparisons: Look for items, ideas, or individuals that are compared with each other. What ideas, individuals, or items are being compared? What similarities are being drawn upon?
  - Lists: When you observe more than two itemized things, then you are observing a list. How many items are in the list? What items are in the list? Is there any significance to how the items are grouped or listed?
  - Cause and effect: Does the cause have one effect or more than one? Have you clearly labeled the cause and the effect?
  - Figures of speech: When images are communicated with words that are being used in a sense other than the normal, literal sense. What word or phrase is being used in a sense other than its normal literal sense?

- Conjunctions: Conjunctions hold our phrases and sentences together. What function does the conjunction serve — connecting (and), contrasting (but), or concluding (therefore)?
- Verbs: Verbs communicate the action of the sentence. What is the tense of the verb (present, past, future, perfect)? What is the voice of the verb (active or passive)? Is the verb an imperative? Who is the subject of the verb? Does the verb have a direct object or indirect object?
- Pronouns: Pronouns take the place of nouns. What is the antecedent of the pronoun?
- Is the pronoun personal or possessive? What is the person (1st/2nd/3rd) and number (singular or plural) of the pronoun?

Essay Questions

Short

1. What are some interesting observations we can make by recognizing comparisons and contrasts within a passage?

2. What are some interesting observations we can make by recognizing causes and effects within a passage?

3. What are some interesting observations we can make by recognizing various figures of speech within a passage?

Long

1. Discuss what can be gleaned by observing words that are repeated in a passage. How can observing the kinds of verbs used in a passage help us to have a better understanding of it? Provide at least two examples.

Quiz

1. (T/F) If you move directly to applying a passage of Scripture from your initial reading, you will have a better understanding of the text.

2. (T/F) By simply observing repeated words in a passage, we can gain some initial insights as to what the passage means.

3. (T/F) Figures of speech, as they are used in Scripture, can be powerful in that they can paint mental images and relate to us emotionally.

4. *"For the wages of sin is death, but the gift of God is eternal life in Christ Jesus our Lord"* (Romans 6:23) would be an example of _____ as it pertains to something we need to be observant of as we read and study sentences.

   a) Contrasts
   b) Allegory
   c) Symbolism
   d) Comparison

5. *"Like a muddied spring or a polluted well are the righteous who give way to the wicked"* (Proverbs 25:26) would be an example of _____ as it pertains to something we need to be observant of as we read sentences.

   a) Contrasts
   b) Comparison
   c) Lists
   d) Cause and effect

6. *"Your word is a lamp for my feet, a light on my path"* (Psalm 119:105) would be an example of _____.

   a) Cause and effect
   b) Comparison
   c) Contrast
   d) A figure of speech

7. _____ are parts of speech that are compared to the mortar that holds the bricks (phrases and sentences) of the biblical text together.

   a) Conjunctions
   b) Verbs
   c) Nouns
   d) Interjections

8. A(n) _____ verb describes the action of a sentence where the subject is being acted upon.

   a) Past tense
   b) Present tense
   c) Passive
   d) Active

9. A(n) _____ verb describes the action of a sentence where the subject is doing the action.

   a) Active
   b) Passive
   c) Present tense
   d) Past tense

10. _____ are important as we read and study sentences; we must identify their antecedents so that we know to whom or what they are referring in a passage.

   a) Pronouns
   b) Verbs
   c) Adverbs
   d) Conjunctions

ANSWER KEY

1. F, 2. T, 3. T, 4. A, 5. B, 6. D, 7. A, 8. C, 9. A, 10. A

CHAPTER 4

How to Read the Book: Paragraphs

You Should Know

- General and specific: The author begins with a general statement, which is followed by the specifics that explain this general thought. What is the overview/summary/general statement?

- What are the specifics that support the general statement?

- Questions and answers: Is the question rhetorical? Who asked the question? Was the question answered?

- Dialogue: Who are the participants? What is the setting? Is the setting public or private? What is the spirit of the dialogue (argument, lecture, discussion)? What is the objective of the dialogue?

- Purpose/result statements: These phrases or sentences describe the reason, the result, or the consequences of some action. Key words: that, so that, in order that, or an infinitive

- Means: When an action, a result, or purpose is stated, look for the means that brings about that action, result, or purpose. Answers the question: what is the means by which something is accomplished? Identify the person or object that accomplishes an action, result, or purpose.

- Conditional clauses: These clauses present the conditions whereby some action, consequence, reality, or result will happen. What is the conditional clause (if)? What is the result clause (then)?

- The actions/roles of people: What is the relationship between the action/role of God and the action/role of people?

- Emotional terms: Make sure to note words in a biblical text that convey feeling and emotion. What words have emotional overtones? What words are relational?

- Tone: Take into consideration the observations you have made, especially the emotional terms, and identify the tone.

Essay Questions

Short

1. Discuss what we can observe by recognizing purpose/result statements in a passage we are studying. Discuss what we can observe by recognizing conditional clauses.

2. What significance do emotions play in a passage of Scripture?

3. Why would it be important for us to determine the tone of a passage we are studying? What could we better determine once we have a good understanding of the tone?

Long

1. Discuss what similarities there are in a crime investigator's observations and the observations we make in studying the Bible. What are some ways we use similar tactics in our approach to Bible study? Provide some examples.

Quiz

1. (T/F) When the biblical author introduces an idea with a general, broad statement it bears no significant weight as we begin looking at a biblical text.

2. (T/F) One significant observation we can make as we are looking closely at a biblical paragraph is to note any questions that the author raises and responds to himself.

3. (T/F) Emotions within a passage of Scripture should be dismissed as we steadily work towards an accurate interpretation of the passage under consideration.

4. (T/F) The Old Testament uses emotional terminology more frequently than the New Testament.

5. One of the key things we need to ask when we notice _____ in a paragraph that we are studying is to ask, "Who is speaking?"

   a) Dialogue
   b) Poem
   c) Speech
   d) Rhetorical question

6. _____ statements describe the reason or the consequence of some action.

   a) Cause and effect
   b) Imperative
   c) Interrogative
   d) Purpose/result

7. It is important for us when studying a paragraph within the biblical text to notice the _____ that bring(s) about a particular action or purpose.

   a) Result
   b) Means
   c) Purpose
   d) None of the above

8. A(n) _____ clause is normally introduced by the conjunction "*If*" and specifies the environment by which some action, consequence, reality, or result will happen.

   a) Conditional
   b) Unconditional
   c) Indirect
   d) Prepositional

9. In reading passages of Scripture that discuss how a believer is to be an "*imitator*" of God, or where believers are described as his "*children*," it is important for us to clearly identify what the author meant by these particular _____ in order to clearly understand and interpret the passage.

   a) Terms
   b) Roles
   c) Analogies
   d) Parables

10. The overall tone of a passage is closely related to the _____ of the text as portrayed by the biblical author.

   a) Voice
   b) Purpose
   c) Meaning
   d) Emotion

ANSWER KEY

1. F, 2. T, 3. F, 4. T, 5. A, 6. D, 7. B, 8. A, 9. B, 10. D

CHAPTER 5

How to Read the Book: Discourses

You Should Know

- Discourse: units of connected text that are longer than paragraphs

- God's message is not restricted to small units of text. Much of the message of the Bible is embedded in larger units of text.

- Connections between paragraphs and episodes: Ask how your paragraph or episode connects with the paragraphs/episodes that come before and after the one you are studying. Look for repeated words and themes. Identify logical connections. Note conjunctions between paragraphs. Pay attention to time sequence.

- Story shifts — major breaks and pivots: Look for critical places where the story seems to take a new turn. In letters pay special attention to verbs. In narrative pay special attention to important choices made by characters.

- Interchange: A literary device that contrasts or compares two stories at the same time as part of the overall story development. Pay special attention when the narrator flows effortlessly between telling two stories. Stories organized this way are meant to interpret one another.

- Chiasm: A list of items, ideas, or events that is structured in such a manner that the first item parallels the last item, the second item parallels the next to last item, and so forth. Search for repeated words, similar ideas and contrasted ideas. Does the end of an episode parallel the beginning? Do paralleling items fall in order? Is there a center to the chiasm, which contains the central idea?

- Inclusio: A literary technique in which a passage has the same or a similar word, statement, event, or theme at the beginning and at the end. Pay careful attention to similar words, statements, events, or themes that occur at the beginning and at the end of an episode. Remember inclusios may span many chapters.

Essay Questions

Short

1. Discuss how we can view and make sense of larger portions of a biblical text. Compare that with how you would approach a smaller portion of text. What are the differences? What are the similarities?

2. Discuss what a "pivot episode" is in a narrative portion of a biblical text. What significance can it provide? How can recognizing it and making clear observations surrounding its given context help us in determining the flow of thought and the meaning that the biblical author is attempting to communicate to us in a given text?

3. How can recognizing a chiasm help us in our understanding of a biblical text?

Long

1. Read through Nehemiah 1:1–11 and make as many observations as you can.

Quiz

1. (T/F) A careful examination of the Bible reveals to us that much of its message is contained within smaller units of text.

2. (T/F) In being attentive to the biblical text, it is important to remember that we are entering into a dialogue with God.

3. (T/F) An interchange describes how a story can take a new turn within a discourse.

How to Read the Book: Discourses | 25

4. (T/F) The Bible is a unique piece of literature in that it is God's Word.

5. A discourse describes units of connected text that are intertwined together and longer than _____.

    a) Chapters
    b) Paragraphs
    c) Stories
    d) Pericopes

6. One of the key observations we need to consider as we focus on a discourse is to recognize _____ between paragraphs and episodes.

    a) Connections
    b) Differences
    c) Comparisons
    d) Contrasts

7. Another significant observation to make as we study discourses is to notice how a narrative may include a(n) _____.

    a) Pivot episode
    b) Interchange
    c) Major break
    d) None of the above

8. A(n) _____ is a literary device that involves comparing and contrasting two stories simultaneously as part of the overall development of the storyline.

    a) Interchange
    b) Pivot episode
    c) Chiasm
    d) Inclusio

9. A _____ describes a certain kind of structured, paralleled set of events, ideas, or items.

    a) Pivot episode
    b) Inclusio
    c) Chiasm
    d) Interchange

10. A(n) _____ is a literary device where a passage repeats the same or a similar word, statement, event, or theme at the beginning and at the end.
   a) Inclusio
   b) Chiasm
   c) Pivot episode
   d) Interchange

ANSWER KEY

1. F, 2. T, 3. F, 4. T, 5. B, 6. A, 7. A, 8. A, 9. C, 10. A

CHAPTER 6

The Historical-Cultural Context

You Should Know

- God spoke through the human writers of Scripture to address the real-life needs of people at a particular time in a particular culture.

- For our interpretation of any biblical text to be valid, it must be consistent with the historical-cultural context of that text.

- The biblical writer: What is the author's background? When did the author write? What type of ministry did the author have? What type of relationship did the author have with his audience? Why is the author writing? What is historical-cultural context?

- The biblical audience: What circumstances does the audience face?

- Other historical-cultural elements: social factors, geographical features, religious life, political climate, economic practices

- Dangers associated with studying background: inaccurate background information; elevating the background of the text above the meaning of the text; evolving into nothing more than a walking database of ancient facts

- Bible handbooks include general articles about the Bible and the world of the Bible. Typically, they also contain a brief commentary on the entire Bible.

- Old Testament and New Testament introductions and surveys contain detailed background information on each book of the Bible as well as an overview of the book's contents.

- Commentaries contain the most up-to-date, detailed information about the historical-cultural context of the book that contains your passage.

- Bible atlases contain maps of the land, pictures of important sites, and helpful historical charts.

- Bible dictionaries and encyclopedias contain information about particular topics mentioned in a biblical text.

- Background commentaries focus on explaining the historical-cultural background that is essential to grasping the meaning of a biblical text.

- Old Testament and New Testament histories provide detailed background information on particular topics you encounter in a biblical passage.

- Special studies in ancient life and culture provide detailed discussions on selected topics. These special studies are similar to Bible dictionaries, but are more narrowly focused.

- Computer software and the Internet provide convenient electronic access to many sources we have already discussed.

Essay Questions

Short

1. Describe the significance of context as it pertains to an accurate understanding of a biblical text. What is the danger of taking a biblical text out of its context?

2. Why is it important to understand the purpose behind why a biblical writer composed a passage of Scripture? How can that help us in determining its meaning?

3. Why is it important for us to understand the audience for whom a passage of Scripture was originally intended? How can that help us to gain a better understanding of its meaning?

Long

1. Discuss some ways that knowing the historical-cultural context of a given passage can help us in accurately interpreting it. Name some potential dangers in studying the background of a particular passage of Scripture.

Quiz

1. (T/F) As we approach our study of God's Word, it is imperative that our approach aligns with how God chose to speak.

2. (T/F) Attention to the historical-cultural context of a passage gets in the way of understanding what God was communicating to a biblical audience.

3. (T/F) It is not important for us as Bible interpreters to know as much as we can about the human author of God's inspired Word.

4. (T/F) One danger to avoid as we are examining the historical-cultural context of a passage is elevating the background of the text above the meaning of the text.

5. (T/F) For our interpretation of any biblical passage to be valid, it must be consistent with the historical-cultural context of the passage.

6. Historical-cultural context is often also referred to as _____.

   a) Foreground
   b) Background
   c) Literary context
   d) Immediate context

7. We need to take the historical-cultural context of the Bible seriously since God spoke to people in _____.

   a) Particular languages
   b) Particular ways of life
   c) Particular places
   d) All of the above

8. The historical-cultural context of a passage involves the biblical writer, _____, and any historical-cultural elements touched on by the passage being considered.
   a) Contemporary audience
   b) Literary genre
   c) Theological principles
   d) Biblical audience

9. Perhaps the most significant piece of information we can gather as we study the biblical author is his _____.
   a) Pre-understanding
   b) Writing style
   c) Purpose for writing
   d) Personal background

10. One of the most fruitful areas of study related to historical-cultural context is _____.
    a) Biblical audience
    b) Literary styles
    c) Comparative literature
    d) Social customs

ANSWER KEY

1. T, 2. F, 3. F, 4. T, 5. T, 6. B, 7. D, 8. D, 9. C, 10. D

CHAPTER 7

What Do <u>We</u> Bring to the Text?

You Should Know

- We as readers of the Bible are not by nature neutral and objective. We bring a lot of preconceived notions and influences with us to the text when we read.

- What forms our preunderstanding: Sunday school, church, and Bible studies; hymns and Christian pop music; jokes; art; nonbiblical literature

- The dangers of preunderstanding — pride: Pride "encourages us to think that we have got the correct meaning before we have made the appropriate effort to recover it. Pride does not listen.

- The dangers of preunderstanding — theological agenda: Theological agenda means that we start into a text with a specific slant we are looking for, and we use this text merely to search for details that fit into our agenda.

- We get to have different thought habits and communication skills from that which is modeled for us on the news networks of our entertainment conglomerates, and we get to be more interested in loving well than in putting someone in their place or making sure everyone knows where we stand.

- We fill in gaps in the biblical text with explanations and background from our culture.

- Our cultural background limits the possibilities of a text even before we grapple with the intended meaning.

- We must submit our preunderstanding to the text, placing it under the text rather than over it.

- Foundational beliefs: While we must let our preunderstanding change each time we study a passage, foundational beliefs do not change as we read a passage. Foundational beliefs are connected to our overall view of the Bible.

- Evangelical foundational beliefs: the Bible is the Word of God; the Bible is trustworthy and true; God has entered into human history; thus the supernatural does occur: the Bible is not contradictory; it is unified, yet diverse

- Preunderstanding: refers to all of our preconceived notions and understandings that we bring to the text, which have been formulated, both consciously and subconsciously, before we actually study the text in detail

- Interpretational reflex: the automatic transportation of the biblical text into our cultural world

Essay Questions

Short

1. What are some presuppositions that we as readers bring to the biblical text? Is this necessarily a bad thing? Why or why not?

2. How can familiarity with a text be both a blessing and a curse in regards to accurate interpretation?

3. What are some ways to overcome the negative side of familiarity with a text? How can we take advantage of our familiarity with a text to better understand it?

Long

1. Using one of the passages of Scripture below, please discuss how cultural baggage can skew an accurate interpretation of that passage.

- Exodus 14
- Exodus 20
- Daniel 3:8–30
- Jonah 1:17
- Matthew 1:18–2:12
- Luke 23:44–24:53

Quiz

1. (T/F) There is no danger in having familiarity with a biblical text as we begin to examine it carefully.

2. (T/F) Most Christians do not intentionally misread the Bible as influenced by their culture.

3. (T/F) It is impossible to be a completely objective interpreter of Scripture.

4. (T/F) One dangerous aspect of preunderstanding is when one comes to a biblical passage with an already determined theological agenda.

5. (T/F) Preunderstanding refers to all that a person brings to his/her study of a biblical text.

6. One context that is often overlooked as we focus on studying the Bible is _____.
    a) Original audience
    b) The reader
    c) Literary
    d) Cultural

7. _____ can be one of the most subtle aspects of what we bring to a biblical text as a reader and interpreter.
    a) Familiarity
    b) Culture
    c) Social norms
    d) Interpretational reflex

8. Different familiar icons from the media, sports, or entertainment can also distort our understanding of a passage. This has become known as _____.

   a) Contemporary integration
   b) Familiarity
   c) Preunderstanding
   d) Cultural baggage

9. Culture can be defined by referring to a combination of family and _____ heritage.

   a) National
   b) Historical
   c) Social
   d) All of the above

10. _____ occurs when we fill in gaps and ambiguities in a biblical text with explanations from our own culture.

   a) Cultural baggage
   b) Interpretational reflex
   c) Textual familiarity
   d) Social norms

ANSWER KEY

1. F, 2. T, 3. T, 4. T, 5. T, 6. B, 7. B, 8. D, 9. A, 10. B

CHAPTER 8

The Literary Context

You Should Know

- The most important principle of biblical interpretation: Context determines meaning!

- By honoring the context of Scripture, we are saying that we would rather hear what God has to say than put words in his mouth.

- Literary context: relates to the particular form a passage takes and to the words, sentences, and paragraphs that surround the passage you are studying

- Literary genre: The word genre is a French word meaning "form" or "kind."

- Genres of Old Testament literature: narrative, law, poetry, prophecy, wisdom

- Genres of New Testament literature: gospel, history, letter, apocalyptic

- We must let the author's choice of genre determine the rules we use to understand his words. To disregard genre is to violate our covenant with the authors — human and divine.

- Surrounding context: refers to the texts that surround the passage you are studying; this includes the words, sentences, paragraphs, and discourses that come before and after your passage

- Ignoring the surrounding context: This occurs when individuals focus on a single verse without paying attention to how the surrounding verses might affect its meaning.

- Topical preaching: Often this preaching method distorts the meaning of Scripture by disregarding literary context.

- To identify the surrounding context, you must see how sentences fit together as a book, in order to communicate the larger message.

- Surrounding context answers these questions: What is this unit's role or function or purpose in the book? What would happen if we removed this section from the book? Why did the author include this section as a crucial part of the whole?

- Steps to identify surrounding context: Identify how the book is divided into paragraphs or sections; summarize the main idea of each section; explain how your particular passage relates to the surrounding sections.

Essay Questions

Short

1. Discuss how context determines meaning. Provide an example from a biblical text where having an understanding of the context provides clues for an accurate interpretation.

2. How is literary genre similar to rules of a game? What significance do these "rules" play in Bible interpretation?

3. What are some characteristics of two of the various types of literary genres that are evident in the Bible?

Long

1. Select one of the passages of Scripture below. Examine its context and provide insights from the context that are significant to determining its meaning.

   - Romans 7:1–6
   - 1 Corinthians 8:1–6
   - Galatians 5:2–6

- Philippians 4:10–13
- Colossians 3:1–4

Quiz

1. (T/F) Context is of such extreme importance in interpreting the Bible, that we can be confident to state that it actually determines meaning.

2. (T/F) Topical preaching can be a valid form of preaching under the proper circumstances.

3. (T/F) The literary genre acts as a kind of covenant of communication similar to a contract between the author and the reader.

4. Literary context refers to a particular _____ a passage takes and to the words, sentences, and paragraphs that surround the passage we are studying.

   a) Cultural context
   b) Form
   c) Surrounding context
   d) Time-frame

5. Literary _____ refers to the types of literature found in the Bible.

   a) Class
   b) Form
   c) Rules
   d) Genre

6. The type of literature found in a passage helps us in our understanding of a passage in the sense that it gives us _____ for interpretation.

   a) Rules
   b) Direction
   c) Form
   d) Function

7. The first danger related to literary context is simply to _____ it.
   a) Ignore
   b) Overanalyze
   c) Misapply
   d) All of the above

8. Recognizing the surrounding context helps us to see how a section of Scripture fits in with _____.
   a) The writer's argument
   b) What comes before and after
   c) The historical context
   d) The cultural context

9. Which of the following is NOT a step we should follow in determining the surrounding context of a passage we are studying?
   a) Identify how the book is divided into paragraphs
   b) Summarize the main idea of each section
   c) Explain how the particular passage relates to the surrounding sections
   d) All of the above are steps to follow in determining surrounding context

10. Which of the following can help us determine a change or a transition in a passage?
    a) Conjunctions
    b) A verb tense change
    c) A location change
    d) All of the above

ANSWER KEY

1. T, 2. T, 3. T, 4. B, 5. D, 6. A, 7. A, 8. B, 9. D, 10. D

CHAPTER 9

Word Studies

You Should Know

- What is the aim of a word study? "To understand as precisely as possible what the author was trying to convey by his use of this word in this context." — Gordon Fee

- The English-only fallacy occurs when a student bases a word study on the English word rather than the underlying Greek or Hebrew word and, as a result, draws unreliable or misleading conclusions.

- To avoid the English-only fallacy, remember that a word in Hebrew or Greek is often translated into English by a number of different English words.

- The root fallacy believes that you can find the real meaning of a word if you can identify its original root.

- The time-frame fallacy occurs when we latch onto a late word meaning and read it back into the Bible, or when we insist that an early word meaning still holds when in fact it has become obsolete.

- The overload fallacy is the idea that a word will contain all of its meanings every time it is used.

- The word-count fallacy occurs when we insist that a word must have the same meaning every time it occurs.

- The word-concept fallacy occurs when we insist that once we have studied one word, we have studied an entire concept.

- The selective-evidence fallacy occurs when we cite only the evidence that supports our favored interpretation or when we dismiss evidence that argues against our view.

- Three basic word study steps: Choose your words; determine what the word could mean; determine what it does mean in context.

Essay Questions

Short

1. Discuss several reasons for conducting a word study within a passage of Scripture.

2. Discuss a plan for conducting a word study in a passage. Why is it not necessary to conduct a word study on every word in a passage?

3. How can identifying a word's semantic range help us to determine its meaning in a particular passage? Why is this important in our word study? How does this benefit our overall interpretation of a passage?

Long

1. Choose three of the common word study fallacies and explain them. Illustrate how dangerous they can be with specific biblical examples.

Quiz

1. (T/F) The English-only fallacy occurs when you base your word study on an English word rather than its underlying Greek or Hebrew word.

2. (T/F) One way that we can determine the meaning of a particular word under study is to see how the author may have used it in another passage.

3. (T/F) The overload fallacy describes the condition where a student attempts to define a word by including every possible sense of the meaning.

4. The primary goal of a word study is to have a better understanding of how a word is used in a _____.
    a) Book
    b) Particular context

c) Paragraph
d) None of the above

5. The _____ fallacy can be described when a student incorrectly believes that the real meaning of a word under study can only be found in its etymology.

   a) Root
   b) Time-frame
   c) Overload
   d) Word-count

6. The _____ fallacy occurs when a student latches onto a definition of a later meaning of a word and attempts to read it back into the Bible.

   a) Root
   b) Word-count
   c) Word-concept
   d) Time-frame

7. If we insist that a word must have the same meaning every time it occurs, we have committed the _____ fallacy.

   a) Word-count
   b) Word-concept
   c) Root
   d) Time-frame

8. If we conduct a word study on a single word and incorrectly conclude that we have studied all there is to know in that particular area of study, we have committed the _____ fallacy.

   a) Time-frame
   b) Root
   c) Word-count
   d) Word-concept

9. Only including the support that backs up our particular favored interpretation of a word describes the _____ fallacy.

   a) Selective-evidence
   b) Word-count

c) Time-frame
d) Root

10. The _____ of a word describes all of its possible meanings.

a) Lexical definition
b) Definition
c) Semantic range
d) None of the above

ANSWER KEY

1. T, 2. T, 3. T, 4. B, 5. A, 6. D, 7. A, 8. D, 9. A, 10. C

CHAPTER 10

Who Controls the Meaning?

You Should Know

- Authorial intent: This approach assumes that the author determines the meaning of a text.

- Reader response: This approach argues that meaning is determined by the reader or a community of readers.

- Authorial intent views a text as communication between the author and reader.

- Question: What does the author mean? Reader response does not view a text as communication between the author and reader.

- Question: What does this mean to me? One of our foundational beliefs is that the Bible is the Word of God; therefore, we read the Bible seeking the author's intent.

- We do not create the meaning. Rather, we seek to discover the meaning that has been placed there by the author.

- Author: When we use this term in conjunction with the Bible, we are referring to both the human author and the divine author.

- Meaning: When we use this term, we are referring to that which the author wishes to convey with his signs.

- Application: When we use this term, we are referring to our response as the reader to the meaning of the text.

- Determining what the author meant: Always remember that language has limitations! The biblical writers used grammar, syntax, word meanings, literary context, historical context, and a host of literary devices to communicate God's message to us.

Essay Questions

Short

1. Why is it important to determine authorial intent?

2. Describe some ways in which language can be limited. What can we do as biblical interpreters to overcome these challenges and understand what the author intended to convey in a text?

3. Describe the differences between a general/universal theological truth and a context-specific theological truth. How can we apply a context-specific theological truth to our lives today?

Long

1. Explain the difference between *reader response* and *authorial intent*. Which is best when reading and interpreting the Bible?

Quiz

1. (T/F) It is important for us to search for the author's meaning in a given text because of serious negative consequences that come from misunderstanding.

2. (T/F) One significant factor to explore as we seek to determine a theological principle from the text is how allegorical imagery is used to communicate its message.

3. (T/F) A criterion in determining a theological principle in a passage is identifying the purpose of the passage.

4. The reader response approach to interpretive position is a dangerous position because at its core it stresses that _____.
   a) The meaning of the text is found in the reader
   b) The meaning of the text is found in the author
   c) The meaning of the text is often inconclusive
   d) The meaning of the text is communicated only by the church

5. In an effort to make a passage of Scripture fit our own preferences, we may unintentionally change the _____ that was intended because of our own dislike of it.

   a) Application
   b) Wording
   c) Interpretation
   d) Meaning

6. The issue of _____ stands at the heart of one's decision about how to interpret a text.

   a) Clarity
   b) Originality
   c) Application
   d) Communication

7. As we study a given text, our interpretive question should look like this: _____.

   a) What is the meaning God intended in this text?
   b) What does this text say I need to do?
   c) What does this text mean for us today?
   d) None of the above

8. _____ can be defined as what the author intends to convey or communicate.

   a) Application
   b) Interpretation
   c) Meaning
   d) Language

9. _____ can be defined as how the reader should respond to a particular passage of Scripture.

   a) Interpretation
   b) Application
   c) Meaning
   d) Preunderstanding

10. In order to determine a passage's _____ in our efforts to apply a text, it is helpful to identify the purpose of the passage.

   a) Application
   b) Meaning
   c) Interpretation
   d) Theological principle

ANSWER KEY

1. T, 2. F, 3. T, 4. A, 5. D, 6. D, 7. A, 8. C, 9. B, 10. D

CHAPTER 11

Levels of Meaning

You Should Know

- Spiritualizing: Our desire to find a deeper spiritual meaning often takes us right past the actual meaning. The Bible is a spiritual book dealing with spiritual issues. We do not have to spiritualize with our imagination.

- Literary meaning: This term refers to the meaning the authors have placed in the text.

- In an effort to make sense of the Old Testament, early Christian scholars developed an interpretative system that acknowledged a "literal" meaning, but encouraged the interpreter to seek out the "spiritual" meaning.

- Allegory: a story that uses an extensive amount of symbolism

- Allegorical interpreters tend to find a deeper spiritual meaning without asking what the symbol might have meant to the biblical audience.

- Typology: Foreshadowing draws from Old Testament passages and then points forward to their fulfillment in Christ. A type is "a biblical event, person, or institution which serves as an example or pattern for other events, persons, or institutions."

- The Bible Code: The authors of this book claimed that there was a special letter sequence code hidden in the Hebrew text of the Old Testament. This special code could predict future events.

- Gematria: Biblical Hebrew uses the normal letters of the alphabet not only to represent the sounds of words, but also to represent numbers.

- Equidistant Letter Sequencing (ELS): This method was employed by the authors of The Bible Code. After uploading the entire Hebrew Bible onto a computer, programmers tell the computer to look for words or patterns of words by selecting equidistant letters.

Essay Questions

Short

1. Describe what it means to "*spiritualize*" a text. Why is it dangerous? Discuss whether or not there should be a difference between a literal and spiritual meaning of a text.

2. How can allegory be used by a biblical author to convey meaning in a passage? How is "*allegorical interpretation*" different from "*allegory*"?

3. Discuss the dangers of Bible codes. What makes them so attractive to so many people? How can we help someone who may have fallen sway to these teachings?

Long

1. What is the difference between meaning and application? How can we derive multiple applications from a single meaning?

Quiz

1. (T/F) Allegorical interpretation is best described as understanding how a particular allegory is used in a biblical passage.

2. (T/F) Typology is a legitimate form of biblical interpretation.

3. (T/F) A type can be defined as a "*biblical event, person, or institution which serves as an example or pattern for other events, persons, or institutions.*"

4. (T/F) An allegory refers to a story that utilizes an extensive amount of symbolism.

5. (T/F) Typology is part of the allegorical scheme that connects the two Testaments together.

6. Trying to locate a deeper meaning of a passage of Scripture that we are studying is often referred to as _____.
   a) The spiritual meaning of a text
   b) The true meaning of a text
   c) Typology
   d) Allegory

7. The _____ meaning describes the meaning that the authors have embedded into the text.
   a) Allegorical
   b) Literary
   c) Spiritual
   d) Personal

8. Old Testament passages that describe things that point to what Christ ultimately fulfills is known as _____.
   a) Typology
   b) Prophecy
   c) Foreshadowing
   d) Promise-fulfillment

9. _____ suggests general Christological connections and significance in an Old Testament passage and does not speculate on the minute details.
   a) Typology
   b) Prophecy
   c) Foreshadowing
   d) None of the above

10. Typology can thus be viewed as _____ in the sense that a historical event or person in the Old Testament serves as a pattern or example of a New Testament event or person.
    a) Foreshadowing
    b) Supernatural
    c) Intertextual
    d) Prophetic

ANSWER KEY

1. F, 2. T, 3. T, 4. T, 5. F, 6. A, 7. B, 8. A, 9. C, 10. D

CHAPTER 12

The Role of the Holy Spirit

You Should Know

- Inspiration refers to the Holy Spirit's work in the lives of the human authors of Scripture with the result that they wrote what God wanted to communicate.

- 2 Timothy 3:16–17 — "All Scripture is God-breathed and is useful for teaching, rebuking, correcting and training in righteousness, so that the servant of God may be thoroughly equipped for every good work."

- Illumination refers to the Spirit's ongoing work of bringing believers to understand and receive the truth of Scripture.

- The limitations of grasping God's Word apart from the Spirit: sin has dulled our ability to perceive scriptural truth; pre-text baggage will distort how an unbeliever reads Scripture; understanding is a whole-person process; unbelievers by definition do not accept the things of God

- When it comes to biblical interpretation, the Holy Spirit does not make valid interpretation automatic.

- The Spirit does expect us to use our minds, proper interpretive methods, and good study helps to interpret the Bible accurately. We can rely on the Spirit to help us grasp the meaning of God's Word.

- The Spirit does not create new meaning or provide new information. The Spirit does not change the Bible to suit our purposes or to match our circumstances. The Spirit brings the meaning of the Bible to bear on the reader.

- Our spiritual maturity affects our ability to hear the voice of the Spirit in the Scriptures.

- Lectio divina: an ancient way of reading Scripture that focuses attention on prayerfully listening to God and allowing him to transform us.

- 5 phases of lectio divina: silencio, lectio, meditatio, oratio, and contemplatio

Essay Questions

Short

1. Describe how the Holy Spirit works in a person's life to help him or her to understand a biblical passage.

2. How much can an unbeliever understand of a biblical passage?

3. How do the Holy Spirit and the Bible work in conjunction to communicate God's truth?

Long

1. Select one of the following passages and walk through the *lectio divina* exercise described in this session. Write a reflection of what this experience meant to you.

- Worship: Psalm 100
- Worry: Matthew 6:31–33 or 1 Peter 5:6–7
- Temptation: 1 Corinthians 10:12–13
- Sin and confession: Psalm 51:1–10
- Freedom from condemnation: Romans 8:1–4
- Abiding: John 15:1–5
- Rest: Psalm 62:5–8
- Renewing of the mind: Romans 12:1–2

Quiz

1. (T/F) The Holy Spirit is all one needs when it comes to biblical interpretation.

2. (T/F) The role of the Holy Spirit is not to author a new Bible, but to bring home the meaning of the Scripture that has already been authored by him.

3. (T/F) As we read and study our Bibles, the Holy Spirit brings about new meanings and provides new information.

4. (T/F) An ancient method of quiet reflective devotional study of God's Word is called *lectio divina*.

5. (T/F) The Holy Spirit expects us to use our minds, proper interpretative methods, and study helps to interpret the Bible accurately.

6. _____ describes the ongoing work of the Holy Spirit in bringing believers to understand and receive the truth of Scripture.

    a) Illumination
    b) Inspiration
    c) Empowerment
    d) None of the above

7. Recognizing how the Holy Spirit works in _____, we know that he works together with the Word and must never be set against it.

    a) Application
    b) Interpretation
    c) Empowerment
    d) Inspiration and illumination

8. The Holy Spirit provides us with a deeper understanding of the _____ that is already there.

    a) Truth
    b) Application
    c) Historical context
    d) Cultural context

9. Although the Holy Spirit does not change the meaning of a passage to suit our personal purposes or situations, he does work with the Scriptures to _____.
   a) Help us grasp the meaning of the text
   b) Transform our lives
   c) Both A and B
   d) Neither A or B

10. Overall, we can say with confidence that the Holy Spirit restores us to our senses as he assists us in interpreting the Word, which is a critical sign of _____.
   a) Salvation
   b) Spiritual maturity
   c) Spiritual immaturity
   d) Justification

ANSWER KEY

1. F, 2. T, 3. F, 4. T, 5. T, 6. A, 7. D, 8. A, 9. C, 10. B

CHAPTER 13

Application

You Should Know

- John 14:21a — "Whoever has my commands and keeps them is the one who loves me."
- Meaning refers to what the author intended to communicate through the text.
- Application refers to the response of the reader to the meaning of the inspired texts.
- The starting point of application is a biblical text.
- How to apply (or live out) meaning: Step 1: grasp the text in their town; Step 2: measure the width of the river; Step 3: cross the principlizing bridge; Step 4: consult the biblical map; Step 5: grasp the text in our town
- The best way to make an application specific is to create a real-world scenario that illustrates the application.
- Contemporization retells the biblical story so that the effect on the contemporary audience is equivalent to the effect on the biblical audience.

Essay Questions

Short

1. Discuss how a believer is to go from knowing how to live out a passage of Scripture to actually living that passage out. Describe some reasons why this may be a challenge.

Application | 55

2. Select a passage of Scripture below and develop specific applications from it.

- Romans 12:1
- 1 Corinthians 13:4–5
- Galatians 6:1
- Ephesians 5:1–2
- Ephesians 6:5–8
- Colossians 2:6
- James 1:2

3. Please choose a passage from the choices below and identify key elements in it that are essential in determining a trustworthy application.

- Romans 12:1
- 1 Corinthians 13:4–5
- Galatians 6:1
- Ephesians 5:1–2
- Ephesians 6:5–8
- Colossians 2:6
- James 1:2

Long

1. Read Jesus's parable of the good Samaritan in Luke 10:30–35. Contemporize the parable by writing a story of your own that retells the original story so that the effect on the contemporary audience is equivalent to the effect on the original audience. Use the back of this page if necessary.

Quiz

1. (T/F) Since the meaning of a given text may vary from reader to reader or situation to situation, we need a reliable method of making sure that the meanings are within the boundaries established by the author.

2. (T/F) One common mistake novice Bible interpreters make when getting to the application stage is making a specific application.

3. (T/F) Application reflects the life situation of the reader.

4. (T/F) Truly grasping God's Word in essence involves adjusting and conforming our lives to the Bible.

5. (T/F) A key step in deriving an accurate application from a biblical text is finding a parallel situation in a contemporary context.

6. Grasping God's Word means not only understanding the meaning of Scripture, but also _____.

   a) Living it out
   b) Studying it
   c) Meditating upon it
   d) Interpreting it

7. Application refers to the _____ of the reader to the meaning of the inspired text.

   a) Interpretation
   b) Study
   c) Reflection
   d) Response

8. When we begin to focus on applying a given text, we need to observe how the _____ in the text addressed the original situation.

   a) Author
   b) Principles
   c) Context
   d) None of the above

9. Critical to coming to an application is noticing certain _____ at the intersection of the biblical text and the original situation.

   a) Interpretations
   b) Theological principles
   c) Key elements
   d) Context

10. One way of developing an accurate application from a biblical text is by creating a(n) _____; yet, we need to exercise caution in that we need to be sure it includes all of the passage's key elements.
   a) Allegory
   b) Parable
   c) Scenario
   d) Metaphor

ANSWER KEY

1. F, 2. F, 3. T, 4. T, 5. T, 6. A, 7. D, 8. B, 9. C, 10. C

CHAPTER 14

New Testament: Letters

You Should Know

- 35% of the New Testament is comprised of letters.

- Informal letters were a routine part of everyday life and were meant to be read only by the person to whom they were addressed. Formal letters were artistic, literary letters designed for public presentation.

- Letters provided a way for early Christian leaders to express their views and minister from a distance.

- Situational: New Testament letters were written to address specific problems or situations related to the author or to the readers.

- Carefully written and delivered: The task of actually writing down the letter was normally given to a trained scribe known as an amanuensis.

- Intended for Christian community: New Testament letters were intended to be read out loud in community.

- The form of New Testament letters — introduction: name of the writer, name of the recipients, greeting, introductory prayer

- The form of New Testament letters — the purpose of the introductory prayer: gratitude for all that God has done in the life of this church; introduce important themes that will be developed later in the letter

- The form of New Testament letters — body: no set format for this portion of the letter, as it addresses the specific needs of each church

- The form of New Testament letters — conclusion: numerous elements can occur at this point in the letter; the most common element is the grace benediction

Essay Questions

Short

1. In what ways did New Testament letters serve as *"authoritative"* substitutes?

2. How would the original readers have responded to the New Testament letters? How should we respond?

3. How can a New Testament letter be misinterpreted by failing to see it as a situational letter?

Long

1. When it comes to letters, we need to be able to trace the author's flow of thought. The first step is to see how paragraphs relate to surrounding paragraphs. Write out your answer to the following questions as a way of gaining experience at tracing the author's flow of thought:
    - How does Philippians 2:1–4 relate to Philippians 2:5–11?
    - What is the connection between Ephesians 5:15–21 and Ephesians 5:22–6:9?
    - What role does 1 Corinthians 13 play in the larger unit of 1 Corinthians 12–14?

Quiz

1. (T/F) In general, the letters of the New Testament are shorter than other ancient letters.

2. (T/F) We should remain cautious in our study of the New Testament letters to not conclude too much from a single letter.

3. (T/F) New Testament letters were only intended to be read by the original recipients.

4. (T/F) The New Testament letters were never intended to be exhaustive systematic theologies, but were meant to apply theology in practical ways.

5. (T/F) Just as a personal letter today serves as a substitute for our personal presence, so did the New Testament letters.

6. Not only did New Testament letters serve as a substitute for personal presence, they were _____ substitutes.

   a) Authoritative
   b) Effective
   c) Specific
   d) Powerful

7. The New Testament letters authored by the apostles carry weight in their instruction, warning, and encouragement because they are writing as _____ of Christ.

   a) Prophets
   b) Witnesses
   c) Representatives
   d) Teachers

8. Occasional/situational letters refer to letters written to address _____ related to the author or to the readers.

   a) Specific people
   b) The culture
   c) The lifestyles
   d) Specific problems

9. Since the New Testament letters are occasional, we need to attempt to _____ the situation that called for the letter in the first place.

   a) Evaluate
   b) Reconstruct
   c) Study
   d) Interpret

10. The form of New Testament letters is very similar to other ancient letters in that they were comprised of an introduction, a(n) _____, and a conclusion.

   a) Prayer
   b) Thanksgiving
   c) Intercession
   d) Body

ANSWER KEY

1. F, 2. T, 3. F, 4. T, 5. T, 6. A, 7. C, 8. D, 9. B, 10. D

CHAPTER 15

New Testament: Gospels

You Should Know

- What are the Gospels: The term gospel translates the Greek word euangelion, which means "good news." Euangelion is understood as: news of political or military victory; news of the birth of an emperor; news proclaimed by or about Jesus.

- Differences between the Gospels and modern biography: the Gospels do not cover the whole life of Jesus; the Gospels arrange events topically rather than chronologically; the Gospels devote a large section to Jesus's death

- How to read individual stories: Take special note of anything that is repeated; be alert for places where the story shifts to direct discourse.

- The most important step when reading a set of stories is to look for connections. Connections include: common themes and patterns, logical connections, transitions, and conjunctions

- Special literary forms in the Gospels — exaggeration: This literary form overstates a truth for the sake of effect to such an extent that a literal fulfillment is either impossible or completely ridiculous.

- Special literary forms in the Gospels — metaphor and simile: Both of these literary forms make comparisons.

- Special literary forms in the Gospels — narrative irony: This literary form uses the principle of contrast — contrast between what is expected and what actually happens.

- Special literary forms in the Gospels — rhetorical questions: This literary form asks a question to make a point rather than to retrieve an answer.

- Special literary forms in the Gospels — parallelism: This literary form describes a relationship between two or more lines of text.

- Special literary forms in the Gospels — synonymous parallelism: The lines say basically the same thing.

- Special literary forms in the Gospels — contrastive parallelism: The second line contrasts with the first line.

- Special literary forms in the Gospels — developmental parallelism: The second line repeats part of the first line, then advances the thought of the first line to a climax.

- Special literary forms in the Gospels — parables: This literary form is a story with two levels of meaning, where certain details in the story represent something else.

Essay Questions

Short

1. How would you distinguish a Gospel from a modern biography? What are their similarities? What are their differences?

2. Explain the special literary forms of the Gospels.

3. How was the content of a Gospel account determined?

Long

1. Select one of the parables that Jesus uses in the Gospels. Study the account carefully. Describe the two levels of meaning within the parable. Share and discuss how you arrived at your conclusion.

Quiz

1. (T/F) When you carefully examine the four Gospel accounts, you quickly notice how similar they are to modern-day biographies.

2. (T/F) Similar in scope to modern historical writers, the authors of the Gospels account for most of the activities of Jesus in written form.

3. (T/F) It is important for contemporary readers of the Gospel accounts to understand what the writers of the Gospels intended to communicate in how they linked smaller stories together to form the larger story.

4. (T/F) As a truthful, master storyteller, Jesus never used exaggeration in his teaching ministry.

5. (T/F) Jesus used parables to convey biblical truth. Parables are stories with two levels of meaning; the difficulty is to know how many details in the story should represent other things.

6. In clarifying what the Gospels *are*, it is important to understand them at their core to be _____.
   a) Theological treatises
   b) Anthologies
   c) Stories
   d) Exhaustive histories

7. As we read and study the four Gospel accounts, we recognize that the authors often employ a _____ layout of Jesus's activities.
   a) Chronological
   b) Topical
   c) Introspective
   d) Personal

8. One of the most significant things to keep in mind regarding application of the truths we find in the Gospels is to _____.
   a) Ask whether or not it is applicable to Gentile believers
   b) Keep the larger context in mind

c) Keep focused on the immediate context
d) None of the above

9. _____ parallelism is where the second line of the text repeats part of the first line, then advances the thought of the first line to a climax.

    a) Developmental
    b) Contrastive
    c) Synonymous
    d) Homogenous

10. _____ are intended to make a point rather than retrieve an answer.

    a) Allegories
    b) Similes
    c) Rhetorical questions
    d) Parables

ANSWER KEY

1. F, 2. F, 3. T, 4. F, 5. T, 6. C, 7. B, 8. B, 9. A, 10. C

CHAPTER 16

New Testament: Acts

You Should Know

- Acts is the story of the spread of Christianity across the New Testament world.

- The Holy Spirit continues the work of Jesus. While the Gospels centered on one person, Jesus, Acts focuses on several key church leaders.

- Luke writes to encourage and establish Theophilus and others like him more fully in their new faith. Acts is a kind of comprehensive discipleship manual, designed to reinforce the Christian faith for new believers.

- The Holy Spirit: After descending in Acts 2, the remainder of Acts is a record of the works of the Spirit through the church.

- God's sovereignty: In Acts we see the fulfillment of the Old Testament as God works out his plan.

- The church: Through the empowerment of the Spirit, the church is a vibrant community where people worship God, care for each other, grow spiritually, and join in the mission of God.

- Prayer: Almost every chapter in Acts shows early Christians praying. The practice of prayer is central to the life of the early church.

- Suffering: In spite of the persistent hardships that the early church endured, the gospel continued to advance.

- Gentiles: In fulfillment of the prophets, in Acts we discover that the true Israel is composed of Jews and Gentiles.

- Witness: The witness of the apostles focuses on the resurrection of Jesus from the dead. And to truly be a follower of Jesus you must be a faithful witness.

- Two interpretive questions: What is the central message of each episode? What is Luke telling his readers by the way he puts the individual stories and speeches together to form the larger narrative?

- Guidelines for determining what is normative: Look for what Luke intended to communicate to his readers; look for positive and negative examples in the characters of the story.

- Guidelines for determining what is normative: Read individual passages in light of the overall story of Acts and the New Testament; look to other parts of Acts to clarify what is normative; look for repeated themes and patterns.

Essay Questions

Short

1. How does the book of Acts differ from the Gospel of Luke? How are they alike?

2. In what way can Acts be understood as a discipleship manual?

3. How can an understanding of the following themes help us to understand and apply the text of Acts today?
    - The Holy Spirit
    - God's sovereignty
    - The church
    - Prayer
    - Suffering
    - Gentiles
    - Witness

Long

1. In reading the various accounts within the book of Acts carefully, how are we to determine what is *descriptive* and what is *prescriptive*? Provide a rationale for your conclusion.

Quiz

1. (T/F) There is good evidence that Luke was the author of both the Gospel that bears his name and the book of Acts.

2. (T/F) The major interpretive challenge we find in the book of Acts is determining whether it should be taken as normative or descriptive.

3. (T/F) As we study the Gospel of Luke and the book of Acts, we notice that the author transitions from theological biography in Luke to theological history in Acts.

4. As we compare _____ there are strong indications that the author intended to link the books of Acts and Luke closely together.
 a) External sources
 b) The opening verses of both books
 c) Other Jewish historians of the era
 d) Inter-testamental records

5. As we consider the manner in which the book of Acts delivers its message, what would the book of Acts be considered an example of?
 a) Poetry
 b) Letter
 c) Prophecy
 d) Narrative

6. The author of the book of Acts could also be considered a _____ as he tells his story for the purpose of advancing the Christian faith.
 a) Storyteller
 b) Teacher
 c) Theologian
 d) Prophet

7. The book of Acts could be considered a _____, designed to reinforce the Christian faith for new believers.

   a) Discipleship manual
   b) Church history
   c) Journal
   d) Biography

8. We recognize the theme of _____ in the book of Acts as we gain a clear picture that God is in control.

   a) Suffering
   b) God's sovereignty
   c) Faith
   d) Persecution

9. Another key observation that we recognize from a study of the book of Acts is how the Holy Spirit works through _____ in order to accomplish his will.

   a) The church
   b) Prayer
   c) His people
   d) The Jews

10. Within the book of Acts we see a natural division in its storyline. In Chapters 1–12 we observe that the leading figure is _____, while the attention shifts to Paul for the remainder of the book.

    a) Luke
    b) Titus
    c) Peter
    d) Timothy

ANSWER KEY

1. T, 2. T, 3. T, 4. B, 5. D, 6. C, 7. A, 8. B, 9. A, 10. C

CHAPTER 17

New Testament: Revelation

You Should Know

- The term revelation suggests that something once hidden is now being unveiled or displayed openly.

- Within Revelation there are indications that Christians are being persecuted for their faith and this persecution is growing in intensity and scope. Most likely Revelation was written during the savage rule of emperor Domitian. Revelation is filled with comfort for those who are being persecuted and warning for those who are trying to avoid it.

- Revelation is a letter: The opening and closing of Revelation resemble a New Testament letter; written to be circulated among churches of Asia Minor; the letters are situational.

- Revelation is a prophetic letter: Prophecy includes both prediction of the future and proclamation of God's truth for the present; the prophecy of Revelation uses the language of Old Testament prophets.

- Revelation is a prophetic-apocalyptic letter: Apocalyptic writing uses a heavenly messenger to reveal God's promise to intervene in human history; God's intervention will overthrow empires and establish his kingdom.

- The images of Revelation create a symbolic world that transforms how the reader/hearer sees and understands the world. Through these images Revelation answers the questions, "Who is Lord—Jesus or Caesar?" The main message of Revelation is "God will win!"

- Interpreting Revelation — preterist approach: Takes the historical context seriously and attempts to understand the book the way the original audience would have, seeing many of the events having been fulfilled in the first century.

- Interpreting Revelation — historicist approach: Revelation is a map or outline of what has happened and what will happen throughout church history.

- Interpreting Revelation — futurist approach: views most of the book as related to future events immediately preceding the end of history

- Interpreting Revelation — idealist approach: does not understand Revelation with respect to any particular reference to time, but rather relates to the ongoing struggle between good and evil

- Interpreting Revelation — eclectic approach: This approach appropriates the strengths of the previous approaches, while discarding the weaknesses of those approaches.

Essay Questions

Short

1. Describe two distinguishing characteristics of biblical prophecy. What are the differences between apocalyptic and normal prophecy?

2. How can we arrive at a purpose of Revelation? Keep in mind the importance of understanding the author's intent as well as how the original audience would have understood the purpose.

3. What is meant by a *"literal"* interpretation as it refers to Revelation? What are we to do with all of the symbolism in this book?

Long

1. In determining the complex literary genre of Revelation, how could it be considered a letter? Why is this significant in addressing the interpretive issues associated with this book of the Bible?

Quiz

1. (T/F) Like other New Testament letters, the book of Revelation is situational. That is, it addresses specific problems or situations in the local churches.

2. (T/F) Biblical prophecy includes both prediction and proclamation.

3. (T/F) Since there are so many details to absorb in the book of Revelation, it is wise counsel for biblical interpreters to focus on every minute detail in order to reach a proper understanding.

4. The book of Revelation is filled with _____ for those who are being persecuted and warnings for those who are trying to avoid it.
   a) Judgment
   b) Comfort
   c) Anxiety
   d) None of the above

5. The book of Revelation is complex. In fact, it combines three different literary genres: letter, prophecy, and _____.
   a) Apocalyptic
   b) Narrative
   c) Poetry
   d) Wisdom

6. A major theme in Revelation is the notion of _____.
   a) Judgment
   b) Retribution
   c) Overcoming
   d) Peace

7. The term apocalyptic describes a group of writings that include a _____, usually given through a heavenly intermediary, to some well-known figure, in which God promises to intervene in human history and overthrow evil empires and set up his kingdom.

- a) Prediction
- b) Divine revelation
- c) Proclamation
- d) None of the above

8. The main element that makes apocalyptic literature so unfamiliar to us is its use of _____.

- a) Images
- b) Prophecy
- c) Dialogue
- d) Divine judgment

9. God uses the book of Revelation to figuratively pause human history and remind believers that _____.

- a) Sinners will be condemned
- b) The world is fallen
- c) This world is not the prize
- d) God will win

10. The book of Revelation uses picture language to emphasize _____ rather than deny or diminish it.

- a) Judgment
- b) God's patience
- c) Historical reality
- d) God's righteousness

ANSWER KEY

1. T, 2. T, 3. F, 4. B, 5. A, 6. C, 7. B, 8. A, 9. D, 10. C

CHAPTER 18

Old Testament: Narrative

You Should Know

- Narrative is a literary form that is characterized by sequential time action; involves plot, setting, and characters

- The meaning of a narrative derives primarily from the actions of the characters; shows us how to live or how not to live

- Literary features of narrative — plot: this literary feature is the organizing structure that ties narrative together

- The basic features of plot — exposition: description of the setting; conflict: can be internal or external; resolution: conflict solved

- Questions to ask: What is the story about? What is the main conflict? How does tension develop? How is the conflict resolved?

- Literary features of narrative — characters: This literary feature encompasses all the people who carry out the action and move the plot forward.

- Viewpoint of the narrator: This literary feature describes the perspective of the story's author.

- Literary features of narrative — comparison/contrast: This literary feature is used to develop the plot and move the story forward by juxtaposing characters or events.

- Literary features of narrative — irony: This literary feature describes situations where the literal or surface meaning of an event or episode is quite different from the narrator's intended meaning.

- The Bible deals with real life and real people. People are complex, and so are the great stories about them.
- Most of the main characters contain a mixture of good and bad traits. And few characters emerge squeaky-clean.

Essay Questions

Short

1. How do we understand and interpret narrative literature? What makes it more challenging?

2. What are some distinguishing characteristics of narrative literature?

3. How can having a good understanding of plot structure within a narrative help us in determining a passage's meaning?

Long

1. How can having an understanding of a biblical character aid us in interpreting a passage? For example, how can knowing that David is a *"man after God's own heart"* help us to understand and derive theological principles from reading about his affair with Bathsheba and his murderous plot against Uriah?

Quiz

1. (T/F) The narrative form of literature could also be called the story form.

2. (T/F) A biblical author mainly uses irony in order to conceal the meaning from the reader.

3. (T/F) As we study the Old Testament narratives, it is important not to systematize God but to let God be God.

4. (T/F) A challenge in Old Testament narrative is that the literary context that must be explored may even be shorter than in New Testament narrative.

5. (T/F) One of the main advantages of using the narrative literary form to communicate theological truth is its ability to connect with people.

6. Four important elements of narrative are plot, setting, _____, and the viewpoint of the narrator.
   a) Style
   b) Genre
   c) Figure of speech
   d) Characters

7. _____ is the organizing structure that ties the narrative together.
   a) Character
   b) Setting
   c) Plot
   d) Form

8. The _____ answers the questions *When?* and *Where?*
   a) Setting
   b) Plot
   c) Character
   d) Point of view

9. _____ is often used in an Old Testament narrative to develop the plot and to move the story forward.
   a) Irony
   b) Viewpoint of the narrator
   c) Plot
   d) Comparison/contrast

10. _____ is a literary term used to describe situations where the literal or surface meaning of an event is quite different than the narrator's real intended meaning.
    a) Irony
    b) Comparison/contrast
    c) Plot
    d) Point of view

ANSWER KEY

1. T, 2. F, 3. T, 4. F, 5. T, 6. D, 7. C, 8. A, 9. D, 10. A

CHAPTER 19

Old Testament: Law

You Should Know

- Moral laws were defined as those that dealt with timeless truths regarding God's intention for human behavior.

- Civil laws were those describing aspects that we normally see in a country's legal system.

- Ceremonial laws were defined as those that dealt with sacrifices, festivals, and priestly activities.

- Old Testament law is firmly embedded into the story of Israel's theological history.

- The law is tightly intertwined with the Mosaic covenant. The Mosaic covenant is tightly associated with Israel's conquest and occupation of the land. The blessings from the Mosaic covenant are conditional. The Mosaic covenant is no longer a functional covenant.

- The Old Testament law, as part of the Mosaic covenant, is no longer applicable over us as law. We must interpret the law through the grid of New Testament teaching.

- The Interpretive Journey, Step 1 — Grasp the text in their town: Study law like you would narrative; pay close attention to where Israel is on their journey of exodus, wandering, and conquest. How did this law relate to the old covenant? What exactly does it govern? What did this concrete expression of law mean to the original audience?

- The Interpretive Journey, Step 2 — Measure the width of the river to cross: We no longer live under the terms of the old covenant.

We are not preparing to enter the Promised Land. We do not live under a theocracy.

- The Interpretive Journey, Step 3 — Cross the principlizing bridge: What is the broad principle that God has behind this text that allows for this specific ancient application? Principles often reflect the character of God, the nature of sin, or concern for other people.

- The Interpretive Journey, Step 4 — Consult the biblical map: Filter your principle through the grid of the New Testament.

- The Interpretive Journey, Step 5 — Grasp the text in our town: Apply the expression from step 4 to specific contemporary situations.

Essay Questions

Short

1. What does it mean that the law was introduced in a covenantal context?

2. Discuss how we should discern which of God's laws are valid today? Provide support for your response.

3. How does having an understanding that the Old Testament is intertwined with the Mosaic covenant affect how we are to interpret it today?

Long

1. Review the Old Testament Interpretive Journey. Explain how you can use it to interpret and apply the Old Testament law.

Quiz

1. (T/F) A large portion of the Pentateuch is comprised of laws.

2. (T/F) The distinction between various types of Old Testament laws was critically important under the traditional approach of

interpretation because it allowed the believer to know whether or not a law applied to them.

3. (T/F) The traditional approach of interpreting Old Testament laws is clearly described in Scripture and is a recommended approach.

4. (T/F) The Mosaic Covenant is a functional covenant today.

5. (T/F) Part of the Mosaic Covenant was God's promise to dwell in Israel's midst.

6. For many years, interpreters traditionally distinguished between _____, civil, and ceremonial laws in their study of the Old Testament.

    a) Territorial
    b) Moral
    c) Covenantal
    d) State

7. _____ laws were those describing aspects that we normally see in a country's legal system.

    a) Civil
    b) Moral
    c) Ceremonial
    d) Religious

8. _____ laws were defined as those that dealt with sacrifices, festivals, and priestly activities.

    a) Civic
    b) Religious
    c) Moral
    d) Ceremonial

9. The best method of interpreting Old Testament law is one that can be used consistently with all _____.

    a) New Testament narratives
    b) New Testament letters
    c) Legal texts
    d) Prophetic texts

10. The Old Testament law is not isolated without context. Rather, it is deeply embedded in the story of Israel's _____.
   a) Theological history
   b) Ceremonial traditions
   c) Civic responsibilities
   d) Cultural history

ANSWER KEY

1. T, 2. T, 3. F, 4. F, 5. T, 6. B, 7. A, 8. D, 9. C, 10. A

CHAPTER 20

Old Testament: Poetry

You Should Know

- The Poetic Books: Psalms, Job, Proverbs, Song of Songs, Lamentations
- The poetry of the Old Testament focuses on our emotional response to God as well as on our emotional response to those who are hostile to God and his people.
- Elements of Old Testament poetry structure — parallelism: This element names when two lines of text are used to convey a single thought.
- Elements of Old Testament poetry structure — synonymous parallelism: This type of parallelism involves a close similarity between lines using words with similar meanings.
- Elements of Old Testament poetry structure — developmental parallelism: In this type of parallelism the second line develops further the idea of the first.
- Elements of Old Testament poetry structure — illustrative parallelism: In this type of parallelism, line A conveys the idea and line B illustrates it with an example.
- Elements of Old Testament poetry structure — contrastive parallelism: In this type of parallelism, line B is contrasted with line A.
- Elements of Old Testament poetry structure — formal parallelism: This is a miscellaneous category of parallelism.
- Elements of Old Testament poetry — acrostics: This element occurs when each successive line of poetry starts with the next letter of the Hebrew alphabet.

- Elements of Old Testament poetry figurative imagery — simile: uses "like" or "as" to draw a comparison; an indirect analogy uses the analogous item without directly stating the comparison

- Elements of Old Testament poetry figurative imagery — hyperbole: a conscious exaggeration for the sake of effect

- Elements of Old Testament poetry figurative imagery — personification: occurs when human features are attributed to nonhuman entities

- Elements of Old Testament poetry figurative imagery — anthropomorphism: occurs when God is represented with human features or characteristics

Essay Questions

Short

1. Over one-third of the Bible is composed of poetry. Discuss some ways in which poetry communicates biblical truth differently than other literary genres. What makes poetry so powerful in its manner of communication?

2. Another element that may be used in poetic literature is acrostics. Discuss some reasons that an author would use this literary tool. Why might you use such a device yourself?

3. Briefly summarize and explain the steps for interpreting Old Testament poetry.

Long

1. Refer to the following passages of Scripture selected from the Psalms. Identify what type of parallelism the author is using in each (synonymous, developmental, illustrative, contrastive, or formal). The author could employ more than one type; be sure to identify all of them. Secondly, discuss how the parallelism used is effective in communicating its intended message.

- Psalm 1:1–6
- Psalm 10
- Psalm 31:1–5

Quiz

1. (T/F) Less than one-third of the Bible is comprised of poetry.

2. (T/F) Poetic literature is characterized by its terseness, a high degree of structure, and figurative imagery.

3. (T/F) An acrostic is a poem in which each successive line starts with the next letter of the Hebrew alphabet.

4. As we seek to understand how to interpret Old Testament poetry, we need to acknowledge the _____ of the images within it and the connection these images make to the emotional dimension of our relationship with God.

   a) Consistency
   b) Function
   c) Meaning
   d) Relationship

5. _____ simply means that poetry uses a minimum number of words.

   a) Length
   b) Abruptness
   c) Conciseness
   d) Terseness

6. One of the most obvious features of Old Testament poetry is its use of _____.

   a) Parallelism
   b) Rhyme
   c) Allegory
   d) Imagery

7. The major medium through which the Old Testament poets communicate is _____.

   a) Prophecy
   b) Dreams
   c) Visions
   d) Figurative imagery

8. A(n) _____ is a figure of speech that makes a comparison using the words *like* or *as* to explicitly state that one thing resembles another.

   a) Simile
   b) Metaphor
   c) Allegory
   d) Hyperbole

9. _____ is a figure of speech defined as a "conscious exaggeration for the sake of effect."

   a) Metaphor
   b) Hyperbole
   c) Simile
   d) Allegory

10. The function of the Psalms is not necessarily to teach doctrine or moral behavior, but to give us inspired models on how to _____.

    a) Live a life pleasing to God
    b) Be a good citizen
    c) Be comforted when discouraged
    d) Sing to God

ANSWER KEY

1. F, 2. T, 3. T, 4. B, 5. D, 6. A, 7. D, 8. A, 9. B, 10. D

CHAPTER 21

Old Testament: Prophets

You Should Know

- The vast majority of the material in the prophetic books addresses the disobedience of Israel and/or Judah and the consequential impending judgment. Prophets use poetry to communicate much of their message.

- The prophets express the deep love of the Lord toward his people and the intense pain that he feels as a result of their rejection of him.

- The nature of prophetic literature — anthologies: Prophetic books are collections of shorter units, usually oral messages that the prophets have proclaimed publicly.

- The nature of prophetic literature — collection: Prophetic books contain relatively independent, shorter units.

- The basic historical context — just prior to the Assyrian invasion: Israel; just prior to the Babylonian invasion: Judah

- The basic prophetic message: you have broken the covenant; you had better repent; no repentance, then judgment; yet, there is hope beyond the judgment for a glorious, future restoration

- The prophets clearly saw the destruction of Israel and Judah. But they also saw glimpses of the destruction of other nations and the judgment of the entire world. The prophets are not always clear when they are looking at near events and when they are looking at far events.

- Some biblical prophecies appear to have aspects of conditionality attached to their fulfillment.

- It is often difficult to determine whether the prophetic figures of speech paint a literal future reality or a figurative, symbolic one.

- Two important questions: How literal are the images that the prophets use to predict the future? Does the New Testament church fulfill the Old Testament prophecies that refer to Israel?

Essay Questions

Short

1. Discuss how prophecy communicates its message to its audience.

2. Discuss how the prophets function as God's "*prosecuting attorneys.*" Provide at least 3 examples from Scripture. How does this literary device prove to be an effective method of communicating theological truth?

3. How is good news associated with prophetic denouncements? What does this say about God's character and his sovereignty?

Long

1. Discuss the "*near-view, far-view*" interpretive problem as it pertains to understanding prophetic literature.

Quiz

1. (T/F) Prophetic literature is perhaps the most difficult for us to understand, mainly because we have nothing similar to this genre in the English language.

2. (T/F) Most Old Testament prophecy deals with events that are still future to us.

3. (T/F) Prophecy finds its power in the arguments it frames.

4. (T/F) The books of the prophets are primarily anthologies, in that they are collections of shorter units.

5. (T/F) One of the major problems that surfaces when we attempt to interpret predictive prophecies is the near-view/far-view problem.

6. A sizable majority of the material in the prophetic record deals with the disobedience of Israel and/or Judah and the consequential impending _____.

   a) Forgiveness
   b) Judgment
   c) Blessing
   d) None of the above

7. The prophets use _____ for communicating much of their message.

   a) Poetry
   b) Imagery
   c) Narrative
   d) Dialogue

8. As we study the prophets, we notice that they serve as God's _____ in that they stand before the Lord, accusing and warning the people of the consequences of their violations of the covenant.

   a) Sounding boards
   b) Ambassadors
   c) Prosecuting attorneys
   d) Spokesmen

9. The covenant in Deuteronomy bound the people to more than just worship of the Lord; it also required _____.

   a) Care for the land of promise
   b) Proper relationships with other people
   c) Legal responsibilities
   d) Moral responsibilities

10. One of the theological principles emerging from a broad study of the prophets is that God desires _____.
   a) Fairness
   b) Judgment against sin
   c) Forgiveness
   d) Relationship over ritual

ANSWER KEY
1. T, 2. F, 3. F, 4. T, 5. T, 6. B, 7. A, 8. C, 9. B, 10. D

CHAPTER 22

Old Testament: Wisdom

You Should Know

- The purpose of the wisdom books: The wisdom books "summon us to think hard as well as humbly; to keep our eyes open, to use our conscience and our common sense, and not to shirk disturbing questions." — Derek Kidner

- Theological foundation of wisdom: "The fear of the Lord is the beginning of knowledge." — Proverbs 1:7

- Starting with this theological foundation and using the salvation story, the wisdom books build a practical theology for living faithfully each day.

- The goal of wisdom literature: the formation of godly character

- The basic approach to life — Proverbs: presents the rational, ordered norms of life; the teachings are norms, not universals

- The suffering of the righteous — Job: the proverbial approach cannot grasp or understand every aspect of life; tragedy strikes even the wise and righteous; in tragedy rely on the Creator

- The failure of the rational to provide meaning — Ecclesiastes: an intellectual search for meaning in life; numerous exceptions to the ordered, rational universe are revealed; meaning in life only found through a relationship with God

- Irrationality of romantic love — Song of Songs: celebrates the wild, irrational, mushy, and corny aspects of true love

- A large majority of wisdom literature is poetic. Parallelism is the standard structural feature of wisdom literature.

Essay Questions

Short

1. Discuss how we need to exercise caution in the way we interpret and apply Proverbs in regards to whether we are to take a particular proverb as *prescriptive* or *descriptive*. What are the differences? Why does it matter?

2. How are we to interpret and apply a passage such as, "*Evildoers are trapped by their sinful talk, and so the innocent escape trouble*" (Proverbs 12:13)? Discuss the challenges we face when we witness evildoers who seem to walk away unscathed by their sin as well as the "*innocent*" who endure unwarranted suffering.

3. Discuss some of the challenges with interpreting and applying the book of Ecclesiastes. What would be some ways in which we can derive theological principles from this book and incorporate them into our lives?

Long

1. Describe how the wisdom books teach theological truths. How is this method different from other literary genres we have observed in Scripture? How is the method effective in how it conveys truth?

Quiz

1. (T/F) A large majority of wisdom literature is poetry.

2. (T/F) Proverbs is probably one of the more difficult of the wisdom books to understand because it speaks to aspects of everyday life like work, friendships, marriage, speech, money, and integrity.

3. (T/F) The practical nature of proverbs makes them applicable to almost anyone.

4. (T/F) Although the wisdom books do not stress the standard

elements of the salvation story, they do nonetheless assume the theological underpinnings of the rest of the Old Testament.

5. The book of _____ presents rational, ordered norms of life.

   a) Proverbs
   b) Ecclesiastes
   c) Job
   d) Song of Songs

6. The book of _____ demonstrates that there are often events that humans cannot grasp or understand.

   a) Proverbs
   b) Ecclesiastes
   c) Job
   d) Song of Songs

7. The book of _____ is an intellectual search for meaning in life.

   a) Job
   b) Song of Songs
   c) Ecclesiastes
   d) Proverbs

8. The book of Proverbs gives guidance for life, addressing situations that are _____ true.

   a) Always
   b) Normally
   c) Never
   d) None of the above

9. The book of Job is difficult to understand because the principles to be learned in it do not _____.

   a) Lay on the surface
   b) Make sense
   c) Pertain to contemporary people
   d) Connect to those who are not suffering

10. Intermediate parts of the book of Ecclesiastes must be understood in light of the entire search and the _____ found at the end.

   a) Hidden meaning
   b) Response by God
   c) Ultimate answer
   d) Further revelation

ANSWER KEY

1. T, 2. F, 3. T, 4. T, 5. A, 6. C, 7. C, 8. B, 9. A, 10. C

Notes

www.ingramcontent.com/pod-product-compliance
Lightning Source LLC
LaVergne TN
LVHW030634080426
835508LV00023B/3368